KEYS *to the* BHAGAVAD GITA

KEYS *to the* BHAGAVAD GITA

A talk by Kriyananda

Based on the Bhagavad Gita
interpretations of
Paramhansa Yogananda

Delivered at Stern Grove,
San Francisco, California
on Sunday, January 7, 1979

14618 Tyler Foote Road
Nevada City, CA 95959
(800) 424-1055
(916) 292-3485

Copyright © 1979 by Kriyananda (J. Donald Walters)
Second Printing, 1990
ISBN 0-916124-15-0
Printed in the United States of America

INTRODUCTION

The lecture here presented was delivered on January 7, 1979, in Stern Grove, San Francisco, as part of a three-day celebration of the birthday of Paramhansa Yogananda. Kriyananda, the lecturer, worked with Yogananda in 1950, while that great guru completed his monumental interpretation of the *Bhagavad Gita*. Kriyananda commented on that work in his book, *The Path: A Spiritual Autobiography*: "Never before had I read anything so deep, and at the same time so beautiful and uplifting.... His book was filled with the deepest wisdom I had ever encountered."*

The public has yet to read Yogananda's *Gita* interpretation. Even when that book comes out, however, Sri Kriyananda's brief presentation in this booklet will serve to highlight some of the salient features of that much longer work.

These days, the reader finds a bewildering array of translations and interpretations of the *Bhagavad Gita* on bookstore shelves. And so it is certainly justifiable to answer a question that must occur to many readers who hold this book in their hands: "What, if anything, sets the *Gita* interpretations of Paramhansa Yogananda apart from all the rest?" Yogananda's own answer to that question reveals the ecstatic joy of one who knows he had received a message direct from God:

---

*Kriyananda, *The Path: A Spiritual Autobiography* (Nevada City, CA: Crystal Clarity, Publications, 1977), p. 403.

"'A new Scripture has been born!' he exclaimed ecstatically after finishing that book. 'There have been many other *Gita* commentaries, but none so all-rounded in their approach as this one. Millions will find God through this book. Not just thousands. Millions! I *know*. I have *seen* it.'"

Kriyananda writes further: "Unlike most philosophical works, this book was fresh and alive, each page a sparkling rill of original insights. With the sure touch of a master teacher, profound truths were lightened occasionally with graceful humor, or with charming and instructive stories, or highlighted with brief touches of new, sometimes startling information.... Best of all, the truths expressed in the book were constantly clarified...with illustration after illustration."

"'I understand now,' the guru told his disciple, 'why my master never let me read other *Gita* interpretations. Had I done so, my mind might have been influenced by the opinions they expressed. But this book came entirely from God. It is not philosophy, the mere *love* of wisdom: It *is* wisdom. To make sure I didn't write it to any degree from a level of opinion, I tuned in with Byasa's* consciousness before beginning my dictation. Everything I said was what he himself intended.'"

"Again the master, smiling blissfully, exclaimed, 'A new Scripture has been born!'"†

A single three-hour lecture cannot, of course, give the reader everything contained in a 1,500-page, God-inspired book. But in his lecture, Sri Kriyananda gives us

---

*The ancient author of the *Bhagavad Gita*.
†Kriyananda, p. 404.

the essential keys by which anyone can begin to understand the profoundly helpful teachings of the *Gita*, as Paramhansa Yogananda uniquely interpreted them.

Names Used in the Bhagavad Gita and Their Spiritual Meaning

Dhritarashtra	Blind Mind
Sanjaya	Introspection
Dronacharya	Guide and stimulator of all tendencies; habit
Bhishma	Ego
Karna (Radheya)	Inclination which seeks happiness, attachment
Kripa	Delusion
Aswatthama	Desire born of past habits
Vikarna	Repulsion
Jayadratha	Body-bound inclinations, fear of death
Somadatta or Bhurisraba	Karma
Duryodhana	Material desire
Pandu	Pure discriminating intelligence
Dhristadyumna	Calm inner light
Drupada	Extreme dispassion
Yujudhana (Satyaki)	Devotion
Virata	Oneness (Samadhi)
Dhristaketu	Yama, negative rules
Shaibya	Niyama, positive rules
Kuntibhoja	Asana, right bodily posture
Yudhamanyu	Pranayam, energy control
Purujit	Pratyahara, interiorization of the mind
Sahadeva	Power to stay away from evil
Nakula	Power to obey good rules
Arjuna	Self control
Bhima	Power of vitality
Yudhisthira	Calm in psychological battles
Kunti	Power of dispassion
Draupadi	Kundalini power
Subhadra	Self-mastery
Abhimanyu	Habit born of self-mastery

Keys to the Bhagavad Gita

Uttamauja .... Vitality or celibacy
Chekitana .... Memory, divine and human
King of Kashi .... Enlightening faculty, intelligence
Shalya .... Material pride
Shakuni .... Material attachment
Dushashana .... Anger

KEYS TO THE BHAGAVAD GITA

The *Bhagavad Gita*—which means "The Song of God" (or "The Song Celestial" as Edwin Arnold translated it)—forms a small part of the longest epic in the world, the *Mahabharata*. The essence of the ancient scriptures of India, the *Vedas*, is contained in the *Upanishads;* and the essence of the *Upanishads* is contained in the *Bhagavad Gita*.

All the essential teachings of the Indian religion are to be found in this very short scripture, which one can read in an evening. But the depth of the *Bhagavad Gita* is such that, when Sri Yukteswar, the guru of Paramhansa Yogananda, was asked by a great teacher of the *Gita* if he had read it, he said, "No—although my eyes have run through its pages many times." He meant "I haven't really understood it yet." And the saint said, "You are blessed to have realized the depth of this scripture."

Every single verse of the *Bhagavad Gita* opens up into such vistas that people have written commentaries on single sentences. I can't even begin to go into Paramhansa Yogananda's commentaries on the *Gita*, because they form a very long book. But I can give you a little of the essence of what it's really all about.

The religion of India is not, as people believe it to be, Hinduism. Hinduism is a foreign name; the indigenous name is *Sanatan Dharma*, which means "the eternal religion." This is not a sectarian or a nationalistic sentiment; anything that's eternal predates country—predates our very planet. *Sanatan Dharma* means that truth which is eternal, and which is expressed in varying ways in all the great religions of the world. So when we talk about the

Bhagavad Gita, we're not really talking about something that is exotic. The name *Bhagavad Gita* sounds exotic; but the truths taught in it are the essential truths of every great teaching, and of every great teacher. To understand the *Gita* is to understand religion.

The *Mahabharata*, the epic in which the *Bhagavad Gita* is set, seems to be a story of rousing adventures and warfare, with many stories that seem more political than spiritual. But the key to it was supplied by Lahiri Mahasaya, our guru's guru's guru. The real meaning of the *Gita* has long been known in India, but I don't know of anyone who brought it out clearly as he did. And what Lahiri Mahasaya said is that each one of us is like a kingdom. (An interesting point here: There is an Elizabethan poet also who wrote, "My mind to me a kingdom is.") And this is exactly the idea of the *Mahabharata:* It's a picture of the kingdom of the mind. Every citizen of the mind is a different psychological trait, and each psychological trait has its own life. We give it that life ourselves; but nevertheless, each trait is like a separate personality. And we find within our own consciousness thousands of these different citizens—some of them noble, some of them ignoble, some altruistic, some selfish, some looking for spiritual truths, and some thinking of how they can get out of having to look for truth. And so we've got this constant struggle between darkness and light going on within ourselves.

HIGH TEACHINGS ARE HIDDEN IN SCRIPTURAL SYMBOLS

The *Mahabharata* is set in history. But we find also in the Old Testament many stories that are historical but that are symbols of deeper realities. Take, for example, the story of Moses leading the people through the wilderness for 40 years. When you look at the map, you get the impression that the Sinai Desert is hardly big enough to spit across! It's certainly bigger than that, but to spend 40 years knocking about in it trying to find Israel seems a bit peculiar. It's really a symbol, a symbol of the soul's search for enlightenment. The wilderness represents the silence of the soul, when we go within the Self. And when we read that all those citizens (again, the same idea) who had been born in captivity had first to die, that they would not be allowed to see the promised land, we have an absolutely perfect spiritual symbol. All those human qualities—"mental citizens"—who have been born in the captivity of delusion—that is to say, those that have been born of ego consciousness: selfishness, greed, hatred, passion, and covetousness—cannot go with us into the divine, or promised land.

You know, it's very interesting: they call it "the land of milk and honey." In a state of *samadhi*, the tongue goes back into a position that locks the energy into the brain. In *hatha yoga* it's called *kechari mudra*. You put the tongue behind the palate and the tongue touches certain nerve centers behind the nasal passage. It seems sort of peculiar, but it's not at all uncomfortable when you practice it. But the practice isn't the same as when it happens automatically when the mind goes into *samadhi*. At that time, in addition to the energy being withdrawn from the body, there is a certain energy that is drawn from the brain down into the mouth. It has a sweet taste, and that energy keeps the body sustained for a long period of time so that one doesn't need to eat. One can remain for very long periods of time in *samadhi* without having to come out. And the curious thing is that the taste has been described—and it seems to me, too, when I taste it—as a combination of *ghee*, which is clarified butter, and honey. How similar to this "land of milk and honey," isn't it? Ghee being butter, coming from milk. The ecstatic state brings that taste into the mouth.

The promised land, in other words, is the land of cosmic consciousness; it's not an outward place on this planet. The saints of all religions have used planetary locations to symbolize spiritual truths, so as, by objectifying them, to make them more real. For example, the *Kumbha Mela* religious festival in India is held at Allahabad, which is where the Ganges and the Jamuna meet; and they say there's a third river, the Saraswati, underground that comes in at that point, too. Well, nobody knows for sure if it's there, but the symbol is that the *ida* and *pingala* energy currents in the astral spine, which are known to yogis, and also the sympathetic nerves that radiate outward in the physical body from the medulla oblongata, both go down the spine on either side, and then join again at the base.

There is this river of energy which takes the mind outward, but the river of energy that takes the mind inward is in the center of the spine, and is known as the *sushumna*. And this is the "hidden river." When the energy is awakened in the center of the spine in the *sushumna,* the *kundalini* rises in the *sushumna* and brings about spiritual enlightenment.

So we have here a symbol in nature of three rivers, at least two of which we know about and the other which may or may not be there. And traditionally it is said that if you bathe at the auspicious time during the *Kumbha Mela,* then you will be saved from delusion; meaning that if you can bathe at this point in divine consciousness, then you will be saved. It's an outward symbol of an inward reality, a symbol that was brought into existence at a time when the whole world was going into a dark age and man was losing touch with the subtler realities. And so in order to preserve those realities, they hid them in symbolic historical or geographical settings.

And so it was with the promised land of the Jews. Remember that the Israelites were "the chosen of God." And whom does God really choose? He doesn't have favorites. The reason He showed a special grace to the Jewish people was because the Jewish people had chosen *Him.* As Paramhansa Yogananda put it, "God chooses those who choose Him." Because the Jews were a dedicated people, they were called the chosen of God. But the real chosen of God are *individuals* who choose Him, who seek God. And the promised land is the land of cosmic consciousness, which is to be found by *all* people, not only by a chosen race.

Those who are dedicated to God, and those who are dedicated to matter, are like two different races in this world. The true races, from a spiritual point of view, have nothing to do with whether you're black or white or yellow, or with whether you're Jew or Gentile. The true "races" have to do with how close you are to spiritual consciousness. In all races we find people who are practically still animals, and then we find also those who are really saintly, spiritual people. Although outwardly they have the same limbs and head and everything else, the differences inwardly, from the spiritual viewpoint, can be enormous.

Well, here then we have a symbol. "Going into the wilderness" means going into the inner silence.

Again, to show you how all these different countries have come up with the same basic truths, look at the Greek legend of Hercules fighting the giant, Antares. Antares had been born of Mother Earth. And so every time Hercules lifted Antares up, Antares would grow weak, and every time he put him on the ground, Mother Earth would give Antares more strength. Hercules realized that he'd never win unless he held Antares above his head until all that energy had gone. So he held him up, and gradually the energy sapped away until Antares died.

Well, this is another symbol—that if we want to overcome *maya*, delusion, we've got to lift our consciousness up into the silence within. We cannot overcome it just by ego consciousness. We cannot overcome it just with New Year's resolutions, saying "I'm going to be good." We've got to bring our consciousness into the inner silence; and in that inner silence, those qualities that are born of Mother Earth—that is to say, those that are materialistic, "of the Earth"—gradually languish and die, and then in that wilderness new qualities are born. You come out of meditation and you suddenly feel kindly. You don't have to affirm kindness; you *feel* it. You suddenly feel happy in a way that you never felt happy before. You suddenly find that all sorts of divine qualities begin to manifest themselves in you—born of superconsciousness, and not just of human, rational consciousness. So those qualities that have been born in the wilderness, that have been "born out of captivity"—which means those citizens that have been born in the desert—were allowed to enter the Holy Land. Those qualities that are divine we can take with us into the other world, but not those that are worldly.

Even Moses was allowed only to see the promised land, but not to enter it. And that's an interesting thing, too. The ego, although it is our greatest obstacle, is also our greatest friend. We can use the ego in the right way to help us. The ego tells us what gives us pain, and what gives us happiness. If we didn't feel, personally, "I'm not happy," or "I am happy," then we wouldn't have the incentive to discriminate and do good. A person who knows that there is good food in a restaurant isn't going to go there unless he's hungry. It's the ego that says, "Oh, *I want* it." As Jesus said, "Blessed are those who hunger and thirst after righteousness."

The ego that aspires for truth, that aspires to absorb itself in the Infinite, is the guru of human consciousness that leads us ever onward. The aspiring ego is the guide that tells us which actions will lead us toward the truth and which actions will obstruct that search. But even the good ego can't enter into the promised land; we have finally to surrender the ego itself.

In the symbolism of the *Mahabharata* and the *Bhagavad Gita*, to touch on it briefly and come back to it later, Bhishma stands for the ego. Bhishma fights on the side of wrong, as we'll see, and he ends up being killed. But he has the power not to die until he surrenders himself to death, and so he's riddled with arrows. Pictures of Bhishma show him with hundreds of arrows sticking out of his body, so that they become a bed on which he lies. This is an artistic exaggeration of that original idea, that even after being attacked to such an extent that nobody could live, he still had the power to give up his own body when he chose. There's a lovely passage when he's lying on that bed of arrows, giving deep teachings to people before he surrenders himself. That is to say, he reaches the point where he is enlightened, where he understands the truth. But no one can kill the ego except the ego itself. We have to *offer ourselves* up into the Infinite. It has to be our own egoic choice to say, "I want the infinite Self, not the little self."

Ramakrishna, who was a great saint of the last century in India, had this experience of being faced with the difficulty of giving up the lower self. Totapuri, his guru, wanted to give him the experience of *samadhi*. But Ramakrishna had been a devotee of God in the form of Divine Mother, and every time he reached the doorway of *samadhi*, which is absorption of the self in the Infinite, he would suddenly see the Divine Mother, and would feel such love—the love of the devotee for his Lord—that he couldn't go through that into the impersonal consciousness. Finally Totapuri took a piece of glass from the ground and rammed it into Ramakrishna's forehead at the point between the eyebrows, crying, "Concentrate there!" Then Ramakrishna mentally took a sword and, slicing Divine Mother in half, went into the Infinite. Thus he realized the highest state of consciousness.

Where there is ego, there will be duality between you and God. You've got to destroy that, eventually, and realize that you are God. Your ego can't be God, any more than the wave can say that it is the ocean. You have to realize that the ocean is the reality of the wave, that the wave has no reality except the ocean. When we see that God has become this I, that God *is* I, that there is no other reality but God, then finally the ego offers itself into the soul, the ego offers itself into the Infinite, and then freedom comes.

It's not easy. That highest and final test is the toughest of them all. At that moment the ego recoils and says, "No, no, no, no—wait!" And they've all gone through it: Buddha told how, on the eve of his enlightenment, suddenly Satan appeared in tempting forms to try to draw him back into ego consciousness. Buddha, with one supreme effort, rapped on the ground and said, "*Mara*— Death—I have defeated you!" And it all disappeared.

Rajarsi Janakananda, Paramhansa Yogananda's chief disciple, was just at the point before he attained that highest enlightenment, and he said that suddenly everything was dark; all this light he'd been seeing during years of meditation and *samadhi* had gone and suddenly he didn't see anything. And there was this strong temptation to disbelieve in it all, but he just kept trying anyway, and after days of darkness suddenly he saw a little point of light, and gradually that point of light came closer and closer until it became Master, then Sri Yukteswar, then Lahiri Mahasaya, then Babaji, then finally, he merged into the Infinite. That same kind of thing we all have to go through.

THE SYMBOLISM OF THE BHAGAVAD GITA

1. Mere History, or Deep Revelation?

The *Bhagavad Gita* is also set in history, but its purpose is to use history in order to express a much deeper and broader symbolism. The main characters of the *Mahabharata* and the *Gita*— Arjuna, Sahadev, Nakula, Bhima, Yudhisthira, Draupadi, Drona and the others— all actually lived on earth. But most of the characters represent psychological tendencies. If you take the Sanskrit roots of their names, you'll find the meanings behind them: anger, greed, kindness, humility, and so on. Each one of them stands for a different psychological trait. In fact, Lahiri Mahasaya drew up a chart showing where all these different qualities were located in the brain.

Even the main characters are fictionalized in many ways. For example, you find the peculiar story in the *Mahabharata* of something for which I don't know of a parallel in any other Indian scripture: where one woman weds several men. You do find cases of polygamy, but I know of no other case of polyandry. It's encountered in Tibet, where a woman will marry a man and all his brothers, but not in India. Yet there is this interesting story, where Arjuna wins Draupadi in an archery contest and brings her home with his brothers, and while they are still outside the house, he says, "Mother, I have brought home a prize." And his mother, without seeing who or what it is, says, "Well, you brothers must be sure to share it equally." Since the word of the mother could not be falsified, they all had to marry the same woman!

The real spiritual meaning of this is that Draupadi represents the *kundalini*, and each of the Pandava brothers represents a different center, or *chakra*, in the spine, and those mental qualities that come as a result of awakening that center. The lowest one is *yama*, the quality of control, the ability not to do the things one should not do. This quality is represented by Nakula. The next one up is *niyama*—literally, the ability of "non-control"; but what it actually means is the ability to cling to right action, to do the things that one ought to do in order to grow spiritually. This quality is represented by Sahadev.

A lot of people with a smattering of knowledge of yoga don't understand what is meant by the awakening of a center in the spine. They think that if you feel a little energy there, you've awakened that center. But the truth is that it's only awakened when all the rays of energy going outward from that center are drawn inward and directed up the spine. A little feeling of energy there doesn't mean the center is awakened; it may be only stimulated. A person could be stimulated by a dream, but that doesn't mean he's awake. When the energy is withdrawn from the body and sent upward, a tremendous flow of energy goes toward the brain, automatically.

The next center, opposite the navel in the spine, is represented by Arjuna. Once that energy is awakened at the navel, or lumbar center—the *manipur chakra*—there comes the quality of fiery self-control.

Then you come up to the heart or dorsal center—the *anahat chakra*—represented by Bhima. When that energy is awakened, you develop true love.

When the center opposite the throat is awakened, you develop very great calmness and compassion. This center is represented by Yudhisthira.

And so we come up to the spiritual eye, which is the positive pole of the medulla oblongata, through which one passes beyond qualities into the Infinite.

You've got two triads here, you see. You've got the three lower *chakras* that represent material desires, and then the three upper centers representing spiritual consciousness. When the energy from the heart is directed upward, your mind automatically is on heavenly thoughts. But when the energy is in the lower three *chakras*, it's automatically on worldly thoughts. You can't pull it out as long as the energy is down there. But to concentrate here (pointing at the point between the eyebrows) draws all that energy toward the divine.

There's even a spiritual astrology involved here. The rising sign in the body is placed, not at the lowest *chakra*, but at the center ruled by Mars: the navel, or lumbar, center. I'm not going to take the time to go into this, but it's a very interesting subject, and one I've gone into in my lessons, *14 Steps to Higher Awareness*. If you study it, you'll understand how external astrology is really an objectification of this inner science.

The symbolism of all the brothers being married to one woman means that the womanly quality, the negative pole at the base of the spine, and the masculine quality, or positive pole at the point between the eyebrows, are parts of the same reality, and have to be neutralized before enlightenment becomes possible. And so the *kundalini* is spoken of as a feminine energy. That energy needs to be "married to" all of the *chakras*—that is, drawn up through each of the centers in the spine and finally united in the spiritual eye at the point between the eyebrows. Hence the symbol of one woman marrying five husbands.

In the story of the *Mahabharata,* one finds a lot of different symbols, all of them meaningful in different and amazing ways. The entire anatomy of yoga is there, and the whole history of the soul's descent into matter. And all of this is captured in the *Bhagavad Gita* as a total picture of where we are, what we're doing here, and where we have yet to go.

2. Keys to Understanding the Gita

Now, the *Bhagavad Gita* is set in this story of a battlefield. Many people think that the setting is literally an historic battle. But true scripture applies on all levels. You can't divide matter from spirit; matter is an imitation of spirit. Subtle, spiritual laws manifest themselves on gross, material levels. Newton's law of action and reaction, for example is a manifestation of the spiritual law of *karma;* the law of gravity is a physical manifestation of the principle of divine love. Every law of physics or chemistry is really an outward manifestation of some subtle, spiritual truth. True scriptures, therefore, are applicable on, and in fact address, every level of life. True scripture, for example, teaches people to perfect themselves materially, as well as spiritually, emotionally, and intellectually. Usually the scriptures apply explicitly to these different levels of reality.

But let's go back before the *Bhagavad Gita,* because the

Gita takes place at a late point in this much broader story. In the beginning we have two brothers, Pandu, who represents the soul, and Dhritarashtra, who represents the mind. Dhritarashtra was born blind, meaning that the mind by itself can't see clearly, can't discriminate. You see, our mental qualities are divided into four: *mon, buddhi, ahankar, chittwa*—mind, intellect, ego, and feeling. Yogananda described the blind mind as a mirror. Imagine a horse reflected in a mirror. The mirror doesn't say, "That's a horse"; it merely reflects back what it is shown. You, standing there and looking at the mirror, see the reflection and say, "Oh, that's a horse." The intellect looking at what is reflected in the mind defines what it sees: a horse, a building, and so on.

Then the ego steps into the picture. Seeing the horse, it says, "Oh, that is *my* horse." Here arises the first real threat of delusion, this separation of things into "mine" and "not mine." But so far the threat is not yet serious.

There is a story of Paramhansa Yogananda when he was still in his teens. I've told this story in my book, *Stories of Mukunda*. His father gave him a motorcycle as a present. Though he owned the motorcycle, he wasn't attached to it, but enjoyed it as if it belonged to somebody else. In fact, he thought of it as God's motorcycle. And when somebody came along who liked it, he gave it away just as freely as if he had never owned it. Did his non-attachment mean that he had *no* sense of ego? In his poem, "Samadhi," he wrote, "I, the Cosmic Sea, watch the little ego floating in me." The fact is, there has to be *some* sense of ego to keep the body going. In a master, however, it's not ego as you and I know it. It's just a tiny abstraction of his infinite consciousness. So in a sense you could say that he had no ego, because it wasn't a limited ego, an ego of body identification.

What really causes the bondage of ego is *chittwa*—feeling. You look at the horse, you say, "That's *my* horse," but then you add, "Oh, how *wonderful* it is to see *my* horse!" Then you're trapped! This is where we find the bondage of ego coming into it, causing us to *like* what relates supportively to our ego, and to dislike what seems to relate unsupportively.

I remember once, when I was a child, how my father gave my brother and me a couple of toys. I was just saying to my brother that my toy was much nicer than his, and he was saying, no, no, his was much nicer than mine, when Dad came into the room and said, "Wait a minute, you've got your toys mixed up." We both very quickly then made the little mental gymnastic of saying, "My new toy is better than yours." You see? That's the way of delusion: the consciousness of I and mine, and of *liking* I and mine.

Well, Dhritarashtra represents the mind, the blind mind. The mind is located at the top of the brain; and Dhritarashtra literally means "that which holds the reins." The mind holds the reins of the senses; it brings everything together in the body. Everything that the senses perceive is brought to the brain; that's how you're able to cognize it.

The mind reflects what it sees, and you know the principle: "first come, first served." You're born in a body, so you're seeing all these delicious ice cream cones, toys, candies—all the things you like. That's what you see first, and so your predilection goes there. In the struggle with delusion, the mind tends to be an enemy, rather than a friend. It should be a friend, but it's clogged up with all of these other impressions. And its offspring, the things it puts out, are of a material quality, they're bound in with the ego. So the offspring of the mind, in the story of the *Mahabharata*, are all these materialistic things. The oldest brother is Duryodhana, who represents material desire. And the spiritual qualities, these higher centers in the spine, are the sons of Pandu, who represent the soul qualities.

Now, this is the sad truth. Some people say, "Why were we ever brought into this condition in the first place?" But my feeling is that we should always try to ask useful questions. Why we were brought here is not a useful question. The fact is, we *are* here. So the useful question is, "What do we do about it?" We've got to get out of delusion somehow. In the story, the sons of Pandu, the Pandavas, are challenged by King Material Desire (Duryodhana), who wants to take over the kingdom that is their birthright. Our birthright, you see, is divine consciousness, and soul-consciousness (Pandu) is the rightful inheritor of this kingdom. But Pandu dies, and his sons (the soul qualities) should have succeeded him. But Duryodhana, who wanted it all for himself, gambled with Yudhisthira. Alas for us! (because this is really our story) the dice were loaded. Shakuni, whom Duryodhana employed, was a skilled gambler who knew how to win by cheating. And so Yudhisthira lost, and five brothers were exiled from the kingdom for 12 years. They were supposed to remain in complete hiding during the 13th year, after which, if they were successful, they would be allowed to come back and take over the kingdom.

Now, I've made the story very brief. In fact, as far as tournaments and dice shooting matches and so on, much more is involved, but the essence of it is this: Yudhisthira represents the soul-quality of calmness; and the tendency, when a person feels very much in tune and very calm, is to think, "Well, I can gamble, it can't touch me." I've seen people do this; they say, "Oh, I couldn't be hurt by that delusion." But the world has its own power; and unfortunately the dice are loaded so that if we go that way, that's the way we're going to get caught.

Those 12 years have an astrological significance. The Indian scriptures say that we progress by 12-year cycles, which actually relate to the cycles of Jupiter. It takes Jupiter 12 years to go once around the zodiac, and if you will look at your life, I think you will be able to corroborate this. I've seen it in many lives, and certainly in my own, that every 12-year cycle represents some stage of spiritual growth—if you're growing! An important spiritual year, anyway; so 12, 24, 36, 48—these are important stages in your spiritual life, and if you make the most of them, you can do much with them.

Kriya Yoga is a means of hastening those cycles by rotating the energy around the spine. Jupiter represents Guru; in fact it is called *Guru* in the Indian astrology. And with the help of the Guru rotating that energy around the spine, one can achieve the same thing inwardly and achieve spiritual growth much more quickly. We can't do anything about how long it takes Jupiter to go around the zodiac, but with the help of Kriya Yoga we can bring this same progress to fruition quickly by working with our own *internal* zodiac.

Let me just touch on that internal zodiac a bit more, so that you may understand it better. Your universe is really inside yourself. The universe outside is only a symbol, as far as you're concerned. Science tells us that there is no center in the universe, but this liberation from a geocentric view of creation frees us also to consider *every* point the center of the universe! Yogananda wrote of his experience of *samadhi*, of universal consciousness: "I cognized the center of this empyrian as a point of intuitive perception within my own heart." Well, was the center of the universe there in Serampore, Bengal? Obviously not, objectively. But subjectively it *is* true. Reality, as Yogananda put it, is "center everywhere, circumference nowhere."

As far as your own understanding of life goes, you are the center of the universe. And it's from that center only that you can grow. So it's legitimate to talk about that as the center of your universe. Everything objective to you is a symbol of these inner truths. In a similar vein, Master (Paramhansa Yogananda) said that the sun is a symbol of the spiritual eye. In astrology they talk of the north and south nodes of the moon. The moon represents the ego. The ego is centered in the medulla oblongata. Once the ego becomes transmuted, the center of self-consciousness in the body shifts forward to the spiritual eye, at the point between the eyebrows. That is why in many paintings of Indian saints and gods they paint a moon on the forehead. It's to indicate that the ego has become enlightened, that the saint's consciousness has become centered here [pointing to the spiritual eye center], rather than at the back of the head [points to the medulla oblongata].

They speak of the north and south nodes of the moon also as the head and tail of a dragon, the dragon meaning the *kundalini*. You remember how often in ancient mythology the dragon is depicted as coiled around a treasure? The dragon is there to protect the treasure. In the Western legend, the only one who was able to kill the dragon was St. George, because he had a pure heart.

The thing is, if we approach that power of *kundalini* with an egotistical motive, it will destroy us—destroy, in the sense that it will give us power for wrong things that will bind us even further in egotism. The *kundalini* is curled around the treasure of our inner, divine power, and when that *kundalini* can be slain, or awakened—either symbol would be valid in this case, the negative slaying of bondage meaning the release of that treasure—then we are able to achieve that state of enlightenment.

The head and tail of the dragon represent the *ida* and *pingala*, the currents on either side of the spine that are magnetized through Kriya Yoga practice. Once the energy becomes sufficiently focused in them, we are drawn into the deeper spine, the *sushumna*, where the inner awakening of *kundalini* takes place.

Well, Yudhisthira—that is to say, our soul calmness—gets shattered, and then our inner nature is banished into the forest of delusion. In this case it's no ordinary wilderness. You're kicked out of your own birthright, your inner kingdom, and you're living in delusion for 12 years, which is to say until you're finished with that particular, outward phase. And it may take a lot longer than 12 years. The Indian scriptures say that it takes some 5 to 8 million incarnations even to reach the human level.

And, given man's capacity for creative ignorance, one may continue for at least as long in a succession of human bodies. I don't want to scare you by saying how long, but I do want to make clear that once one comes to the point of knowing that he wants God, he is a very, very long way along—almost out, in fact, by comparison with where he has been. This is the truth.

One time Norman (a fellow disciple) said to Yogananda, "I don't think I have very good *karma*, Sir." (We all go through this sort of thing from time to time!) Master looked at him and said, "Remember this: It takes very, *very*, VERY good *karma* even to want to know God." You see, it takes a long time for the soul to realize that what it wants cannot be found outside itself, because there are so many ways of getting into mischief. If you don't make it in America, how about Turkey? And if you don't make it as an opera star, well, what about sculpture, or business, or something.

In the *Gita* you find the statement, "Our army is difficult to count, but their army is easy to count"—"our army" meaning the negative side, which I'll have to explain in more detail later. The faults that we can get into are myriad, but the virtues are few—few because, the closer you get to simplicity, the more you have everything in one or two or three basic principles. So the way of divine love is one, but the paths of passion can be counted in millions. You can be infatuated with all kinds of things. So the army of the Kauravas was many, while the army of the Pandavas, by comparison, was few.

There are some wonderful spiritual stories and symbols in the *Mahabharata*; it's a great, great scripture, although you've got to read it with insight. To understand it you can't just take it as a good story—which it certainly is; but you've got to take it down to a deeper level. There is this one part, for example, where Krishna gives Duryodhana (King Material Desire), and Arjuna (fiery self-control, the main warrior of the Pandavas) a choice. He says, "You can either have all my army, with millions of soldiers, or you can have me. But if you have me, I won't fight. I'll just be with you at your side."

Arjuna said he wanted Krishna, and Duryodhana was congratulating himself on his good fortune, because he had all these millions of soldiers while Krishna had said he wouldn't even *help* poor Arjuna. But Arjuna had the wisdom to know that where God was, there victory had to be. (There is this Indian saying, the motto of the *maharaja* of Cooch Behar: *"Yato dharma, tato jaya."* "Where there is *dharma*, or righteousness, there is victory.") This is what happens in the *Bhagavad Gita*: Just because Krishna was on their side, they finally won.

The truth is, God doesn't seem to help us. I mean, when you see help with worldly eyes, you see somebody coming up with money, or a checkbook, or a hammer to help you. But you pray to God, and you think, "Well, where is He?" But what happens is that He works *through* you, and you suddenly find that you've got the power to do it, or through others, and suddenly you find it done. We always expect that if He's going to answer us at all it's going to be in a great vision, or that He'll come out and blast our enemies. But it doesn't work that way. And yet somehow it does work. It's peculiar, but it happens. It may happen objectively, too. In many miraculous ways, devotees find their prayers answered. But always it's in such a way that you sort of scratch your head and say, "Was that really Him looking after me, or was it a coincidence?" He doesn't declare Himself "from the clouds"; it's always in subtle ways.

And so if you cling to God, you may not see *how* He is working, but you will find that you always come out ahead. This is one of the lovely truths that is expressed in the *Bhagavad Gita*: "O Arjuna, know this for a certainty: My devotee is never lost." When you cling to God, He will always bring you out in time. Just cling. Don't give up. He may sometimes test you, perhaps mightily, perhaps only playfully. It doesn't always seem playful to us, at first! But He will not let you down; He *cannot* let you down if you cling to Him. It's an infallible rule, a law of life.

And so in this initial story we find that Yudhisthira sacrifices the kingdom and is dismissed for "12 years"— the cycle of time that he passes through before he begins to wake up. This is what has happened to us, too. At some point in the past we gambled, and we were dismissed into *maya*, banished out of our own divine kingdom. It was *our* doing. We were dumb! (laughter) And so we have wandered for a while. But now we've reached the point where we say, "It's time my exile were over. I want to come back, and I want to reclaim my inner kingdom."

But by then, of course, Duryodhana (King Material Desire) and all his cohorts are firmly entrenched. In the fitness of things, they should be honorable. At least they should say, "Sure, you can have your half of the kingdom, and we'll keep the other half." But material desire won't have any such harmonious compromise.

Perhaps you've seen this happen in married life—

maybe even in your own family—that if a wife or a husband gets on the spiritual path, and the spouse isn't on the path, although in the fitness of things the spouse who isn't should say, "Well, that's all right. You meditate, and we'll still have our marriage," what you find almost invariably is that there is jealousy, that the husband will be jealous of his wife for the time she spends meditating. There comes friction.

Jesus said, "I didn't come to bring peace, but to bring a sword. I came to set father against son, and mother against daughter."

It was not that he was spreading discord, but simply that the truths he was teaching presented an "either/or" proposition. We can't have both. Our subconscious material desires recognize a lot sooner than our conscious ego does, that it is a fight to the finish. And so material desire comes in and says, as Duryodhana says in the Mahabharata, "I will not give them as much ground as could be covered by a piece of straw." And so at that point a righteous war developed. It was the Pandavas' birthright to rule. Moreover, the people of the country wanted it. So the brothers had to fight to reclaim their lost property.

They would have been just as happy to rule just a little kingdom. Many people, likewise, would be very happy to give just a little bit of time to God, and then go out and enjoy the world. But material desire won't let them. They are going to have to fight for their time to meditate. They're going to have to struggle to claim that thought of devotion, that thought of God. Sooner or later, as a result of that conflict, King Material Desire has to go. There's no other way out.

Well now, I don't usually teach that way, do I? I bargain. I say, "Well, five minutes...after all, just get the taste for it." (laughter) "Come on, give it a try." (laughter) But the fact is, if you give it a try...How do you get to be an alcoholic? Well, you take a sip, and then another sip; then pretty soon you're sipping all the time, and so it is that if you get a little taste of inner joy, you'll want more. I don't want to scare people who are new on the path. But the truth is that your own desire for that peace will become so powerful that you'll finally realize that it alone is real, and the other totally unreal. You will acquire this consciousness quite spontaneously, on your own. Nobody's ever going to impose this understanding on you. You'll make that comparison yourself between wisdom and delusion. In effect, you'll say, "Why cling to ten dollars, when I could have a million?"

At Ananda once we set a trap out for a raccoon that was getting into people's food. The next morning we found the raccoon, but it hadn't been caught in the trap; it had reached through the bars of the trap and grabbed the food. Imagine, it was so attached to that food that it wouldn't let go, even when people came and got it! We carried it away, trap and all, still clinging to the food. It was just as trapped by its own greed as if we'd actually caught it. (laughter) Well, it's a marvelous metaphor, isn't it? Our attachment to this world is just like that. We don't have to be attached, it's not necessary; but we cling, and so we get caught.

Wouldn't it be absurd not to sacrifice a piece of food that you couldn't even eat, for freedom? I mean, the raccoon could easily have relinquished the food, which it couldn't get anyway, and run away. But because of its attachment it was caught.

Well, we can't ever have anything, really, through the senses. Our enjoyment is vicarious; we aren't really eating that food, our body's eating that food. We're in the brain; it's just an idea in the mind that something's happening. It's all feeding somebody else. It's not our real Self. And the same is true for every human satisfaction. As long as it's through the senses, it's vicarious.

The real joy...I know when I first heard the sound of *OM*, I thought with such a thrill that it was the only sound I'd ever heard that I could listen to for all eternity, and never get tired of it. Because all music, even the most lovely symphony, is still *out there*; but *OM* is your own *Self*, it's the music of your own being. It's playing on the heartstrings of your consciousness. And so it is that as you meditate, you feel that joy, and you realize that that's the only reality. That's how you come to the point where it's just one or the other: Finally you just don't want the other.

There is this constant struggle between your desires, and knowing what you *ought* to do—not because the scriptures say so, but because from your own heart you know that this alone will give you true joy. These opposing choices are in constant conflict with one another. While a part of you is saying, "I want freedom, I want joy, I want the higher Self," the other part is saying, "Oh, no, not that! Oh, no, please let me hang onto this!" And so the struggle goes on.

And now we come to the actual beginning of the *Bhagavad Gita*, when Dhritarashtra—at a distance, because he's blind and can't take part in the battle, and anyway he's an old man by now—asks Sanjaya, who represents the introspective faculties, "My children, the Kurus and the Pandavas, what did they on this field of battle?" Later in the *Bhagavad Gita* it says clearly that this body is the battle field, the *karma kshetra*, the field of action. And so Dhritarashtra is really talking about the body.

Another strong clue to the fact that the battlefield is symbolic is this: Sanjaya had divine sight, so that he was able to see clearly what was happening in the distance; and he was telling Dhritarashtra, just like a TV, what was going on. And here is one of these little clues that are put there for the discriminating to see. If it had really been a story about a battle, with no symbolism intended, Dhritarashtra would not have asked, "What *did* they?" but, "What *are they doing?*" The reason for this difference is that Byasa, the author of the *Bhagavad Gita*, wanted to show us that he was talking about introspection.

Sanjaya, the introspective faculty, is looking at the battle. You don't introspect while you're fighting, do you? You don't have time to introspect. But afterwards you stop and think, "Who won? How did it go?" The two sides are ranged against one another, the good and the bad; and after every battle with greed, with anger, with passion, with whatever it is you look back and say, "Well, I wonder how I did? Which side won?" If the good side won, you feel good; and if the bad side won, you feel dejected. You can't get out of that. It's not just a matter of the values that were taught you by society; it's a question of your own soul knowledge.

Anything that limits consciousness causes pain. Anything that expands it causes joy. And so this teaching is saying that anything that we do that goes against our higher nature causes our consciousness to shrink. Therefore you will know, after introspection, "I blew that one," or, "Oh, how good I feel!"

You may have noticed, if ever you've been to a golf club, or on the ski slopes, or wherever people are engaged in some form of physical exercise, how the people there tend to talk loudly and tell jokes. Their laughter is of an egoic sort, to be sure, and yet there's also a certain genuine joy in it. That joy springs from the thought, "I'm mastering my body." Go out onto the ski slopes sometime and note how the people there call to one another confidently: "Come on, try this slope!" They feel so good! It's all due to the thought, "I'm gaining control of my body!"

The mere thought of self-control brings joy. The mere thought gives a sense of victory. We all, without even always knowing about it, have this battle going on inside, in some of us more consciously than in others. We feel good when the right side wins, and badly when the wrong side wins. The trouble is, we're on both sides!

So Sanjaya represents the introspective faculty, and Sanjaya sees Arjuna go between the two armies, and look at the two sides. Before that there are certain very interesting passages. In the translation by Christopher Isherwood, the whole first chapter is dismissed as just a catalog of names; but in fact there's a lot of spiritual teaching in those early passages. Let me read them to you now:

"Dhritarashtra said, 'Sanjaya, assembled on the holy field of Kurukshetra, eager for battle, what did my children and the children of Pandu do?' Sanjaya said, 'At that time, seeing the army of the Pandavas drawn up for battle and approaching Dronacharya, Prince Duryodhana spoke these words: "Behold, Master, the mighty army of the sons of Pandu arrayed for battle by your talented pupil Dhristadumnya, the son of Drupada."

[I'm not going to go into all of these words. Each one of them, however, represents a psychological trait.]

""'There are in this army heroes wielding mighty bows and equal in military prowess to Bhima and Arjuna, such as Satyaki and Virata and the Maharathi (great car-warrior) Drupada; Dhrishtaketu, Chekitana, and the valiant king of Kashi, and Purujit, Kuntibhoja, and Shaibya, the best of men, and mighty Yudhamanyu, and valiant Utamauja, Abhimanyu, the son of Subhadra, and the five sons of Draupadi, all of them Maharathis (great car-warriors).'"

""'O best of Brahmins, know them also who are the principal warriors on our side, the generals of my army. For your information I mention them below:

""'Yourself, and Bhisma, and Karna,...'"' and so on.

And then he goes on...this translation is wrong, so I've corrected it according to the way Master wrote it: "This army of ours, fully protected by Bhishma, is difficult to count, while that army of theirs, guarded in every way by Bhima, is easy to count." Meaning, again, "Ours is so numerous, that's why it's difficult to count—the bad qualities are so numerous." Then he says, "Therefore, do everything you can to guard Bhishma."

Now, remember who Bhishma is? Bhishma represents the ego. And King Material Desire says, "By all means, do what you can to protect the ego. As long as the ego's safe, we're safe. As long as there's ego we can have material desire, we can have everything. But if ego goes, then we're all sunk." (laughter) Well then, here's a very interesting section. He was getting a little bit worried and fearful, you see, but: "Then the grand old man of the Kaurava race, their glorious grand uncle Bhishma, cheering up Duryodhana, roared terribly like a lion and blew his conch."

Now, physiologically, the medulla oblongata, at the base of the skull, operates the heart and the breath. The ego is centered in the medulla. The conch of the ego is the breath. (The lung even looks somewhat like a conch shell!) But what happens here is that as you go into deep meditation you begin to hear inner sounds. You may hear harp sounds, emanating from the lumbar center, or bell sounds, emanating from the heart center, or other heavenly music—sounds that draw you into the inner heaven, such that your breath ceases.

In deep meditation one goes beyond breathing; the breath becomes still. Then suddenly the ego says, "What's happening? I'm not breathing! I'm slipping away from body consciousness. I may get lost!" In your anxiety you breathe again. So what we see here is Bhishma trying to cheer up Duryodhana—the ego, you see, cheering up material desire—by breathing again. And soon as that happens, then, as the *Gita* puts it, "Conches, kettle drums, tabors, drums, and trumpets suddenly blared forth and the noise was tumultuous."

The battle hasn't even started, really; the author is just depicting some of the preliminary struggles.

"Then, seated in the glorious chariot drawn by white horses, Sri Krishna and Arjuna blew their celestial conches." As you dip into meditation, you begin to hear these sounds, these celestial sounds. "Sri Krishna blew his conch named Panchajanya; Arjuna, his conch called

Devadatta, while Bhima blew his mighty conch Paundra, and Yudhisthira blew his conch, Anatavijaya." You see, each one of these is representing a different *chakra;* Krishna representing the OM itself, and then each one of these centers with its own different sound. The energy emanating from the lowest *chakra,* the coccyx center or *muladhara,* is of a bee, a bumble bee; or, if you hear it imperfectly, it may sound like a motor, but nonetheless an absorbing, inward kind of sound.

One time Yogananda was sitting in a room with his disciple Dr. Lewis. Dr. Lewis was at the other end of the room, and Master said, "Listen." That sound of his coccyx was so strong that Dr. Lewis could hear it all the way across the room.

When you stimulate that center, that's the sound that comes. The next center up is Krishna's flute, a flute sound. That's why we talk of Krishna's flute calling devotees from the countryside into the village. So you see, even though, when the energy goes outward from these centers, the consciousness is material, yet when the energy turns inward they become spiritual and enlightening. The energy from the lumbar center, the *manipur chakra,* makes a sound as of a plucked string instrument—the *vina,* they call it in India, but we would liken it to a harp sound. The heart center sounds like a deep gong bell; the throat center (the *vishudha chakra,* or cervical center) is like the sound of wind in the trees, a very soothing and expanding sound. And the medulla is a combination of all of these; the sound here could be thought of as a bursting sea, and that approaches very near now to OM.

Each one of these centers has a particular sound, and

that's what is being described here allegorically as warriors blowing their conches. "Sahadeva and others blew theirs respectively, and the terrible sounds echoed through heaven and the earth, wrenching the hearts of Dhritarashtra's sons." At the point when you start to hear those sounds, material desire starts to grow fainthearted; you lose the taste for anything but those sounds. The trouble is, habit comes in; and unfortunately, as we see in the *Mahabharata*, habit ranges on the wrong side. Dronacharya (habit) was the teacher of both armies. But in the struggle between matter and spirit, habit tends to support the outer, more familiar tendencies, until we develop very strong spiritual habits.

Dhritarashtra's race becomes discouraged, but then habit comes in and gives strength to those old tendencies, and so they go out to battle again. One after another, a succession of psychological traits takes over, leading the armies of material desire against the armies of the soul.

We return now to the good side: "Now, O Lord of the Earth, seeing your sons arrayed against him, and when missiles were ready to be hurled, Arjuna, the son of Pandu..." There is something that is not written in this translation, but that Master wrote: "...whose flag had the monkey emblem." As the raccoon represents greed, so the monkey represents mental restlessness. Thus, to "hoist the monkey emblem" means to raise the banner of restlessness—to control restlessness, resolving, "I refuse to be restless anymore. I will go into the Self."

In India they have a class of *sannyasis*, or monks, who carry a *danda*, a long staff, wherever they go. This staff signifies the spine; they carry it as a reminder to live always in the spine. Now, the battle of Kurukshetra takes place not only generally in the body, but more particularly in the spine. "The son of Pandu, whose flag had the monkey emblem, took up his bow." The bow in this case means the spine. The front of the body is like the wooden part of the bow, and the string is the spine itself. When you unstring the bow, the wooden part straightens up, comparable to the body's slumping forward. When you hold your body erect in meditation, the spine is straight, the front of the body comes forward, like an arched bow. Then you're ready for action, you're ready for battle. That's why in this instance the body is described here as a bow.

Arjuna says to Krishna, "Krishna, place my chariot between the two armies, and keep it there until I have carefully observed these warriors drawn up for battle, and have seen with whom I have to engage myself in this fight. I will scan the well-wishers in this war of evil-minded Duryodhana, who have assembled here and are ready for the battle." Sanjaya said, "O King, thus addressed by Arjuna, Sri Krishna placed the magnificent chariot between the two armies, in front of Bhishma, Drona, and all the kings, and he said, 'Arjuna, behold these Kauravas assembled here.'"

And so, what happened? After all, I did say that spiritual truth manifests itself on all levels; and so in one way, that battle goes on outwardly all the time. When you have a businessman who's offered a crooked means of making a hundred thousand dollars quickly, you have that same battle—"Shall I get rich quick by dishonest means, or shall I cling to the truth, even though I don't get that money?" Offered the chance for fame and success at the expense of someone else, shall I take that chance, or shall I say, "No, I will cling to the truth, I will not use dishonorable means of achieving anything, even glory."

Again and again, we find these battles in our lives. And it wouldn't hurt always to play it as if you were standing a little bit behind yourself, watching what it is you do. Always keep a part of your mind a bit separate, observing your actions. But mostly you'll find that this observation, this time for introspection, will occur *after* the battle has been fought—when you look back and say, "Which side won?" Nonetheless, always try to observe yourself. Soon you'll see that it really is a battle. Be prepared to do spiritual battle in your life.

The subtler meaning of this battle is that when you go deep in meditation and your energy withdraws into the spine, into the *sushumna*, that's when the real struggle begins, because there you can see the battle much more clearly. In fact, the battle may even become objectified in visions. St. Anthony of the Desert told how demons would appear to him, saying, "You don't want to be here praying. Go back to the city—have fun!" Devananda, one of the monks that I've mentioned in *The Path*, told me that soon after he arrived at Mt. Washington he heard a voice in meditation one day, saying, "You don't want to live here. Go back." Whether it's objectified in a vision or not, it's the subconscious tendencies expressing themselves, the demons of your own mind telling you how nice it is after all, to live in this world. And these traits become more clearly manifested, once that energy has been withdrawn into the spine.

Perhaps it would help to look at it this way. You see a

stained glass window on a grey day and, although there are a lot of colors in it, they may all look more or less the same. But when the sun shines through the window, the colors become brilliant. I've observed that as people develop spiritually, they may manifest certain negative qualities to a ridiculous degree—much more so than ordinary people. You wonder, "They're spiritual—so what is this?" (laughter) I saw one saintly man, a person for whom I had a great deal of respect, even reverence, act almost childish sometimes—in little ways, to be sure. But I'd think, "My goodness, even I'm not like that, and I'm just a spiritual child compared to him." You see, as the energy in the body becomes strong, it highlights everything—bad traits as well as good. And, of course, until we see them highlighted, we can't deal with them.

So it's not as if those people were necessarily going backwards, spiritually. Rather, it's that they're getting more energy; whereas in an average, unenlightened human being no quality is very strong. I never heard people in Scarsdale say, "It's wonderful!" They'd say, "It's nice." (laughter) The average person's enthusiasm is limited to, "Yeah, maybe we *ought* to go." (laughter) All his qualities are sort of medium.

I mentioned a story in *The Path* about Dr. Kennell, who was a very sincere and good man, a disciple of Master. Master, before his services, would cry, "How is everybody? Awake and ready!" like this, with much energy to get people stirred up. (You see, you have to be fully conscious, fully aware, before you can achieve superconsciousness.) Dr. Kennell, who, though a good man, didn't have Master's level of energy, told me before the first service I heard him give, "I like to keep things on a more moderate level." (laughter) So after he came out, he said, "I trust that everyone present this morning is feeling awake and ready." (laughter) You see, how, with diminished energy, one tends to tone everything down?

Geniuses seem, to moderate eyes, to go to extremes. Most people can't understand such dynamic energy. They can't stand to be around greatness for that reason; still less can they stand to be around saints. Saints have too much energy for them. Ordinary people find them exhausting. That's why Badhuri Mahasaya—the levitating saint that Master mentioned in the *Autobiography of a Yogi*, you remember?—discouraged people from coming to see him too easily. As he explained, "It's not for my sake; it's for their sake."

Well, this is the kind of energy that we need to develop. The trouble is, of course, that most people, rather than coming to the point where they rise above obstacles, hope vaguely that they may get away with sinking below them. (laughter) But it doesn't work.

Well, here is the predicament: When that energy becomes very strong in the spine, you see all your own qualities more clearly. You see what you have to work with. When you can objectify your faults, some of them may seem terrible, but remember, this is also the point at which you can deal with them and ultimately get rid of them altogether.

So in the deep spine, you see, Arjuna actually represents the point between the two armies, doesn't he?—the navel *chakra* of self-control, the lumbar or *manipur* center, in the middle between the two armies. When the energy comes to that point, you observe those qualities that are trying to pull you downward, and those that are pulling you upward; and you analyze the two, to see how they are pitted against each other.

"Arjuna saw stationed there in both armies, uncles and grand uncles, teachers and maternal uncles, brothers and cousins, sons, grandsons, friends, fathers-in-law, well-wishers as well. Seeing all those relatives of his present there he was possessed by extreme pity, and he uttered these words in sadness: 'O Krishna, at the sight of these kinsmen arrayed in longing to fight one another, my limbs give way, my mouth is parched, my frame shakes and my hair stands on end. My bow, Gandiva, drops from my hand.'"

"Drops from his hand" means he slumps forward, his meditative pose breaks, as he thinks, "Oh, I can't meditate, it's too difficult." What he's seeing is that even those qualities that are his enemies are yet his own relatives—members of his own psychological family. That's the trouble we're all in. In principle I may be definitely opposed to, or at least critical of, negative qualities, but when it comes to *my* negative qualities—well, that's another story. (laughter) I may say that greed, generally, is bad, but when it comes to liking curries, that's another story. (laughter)

And so Arjuna is saying, "These are my own relatives. How can I kill my relatives?" They're a part of his own consciousness. To get rid of bad habits would seem to mean killing a part of one's own nature.

Arjuna goes on: "My skin burns all over, my mind is reeling." Actually, the skin's burning is one symptom of the inner conflict we've been describing. I mentioned in *The Path* how Yogananda was walking around the grounds of his desert retreat, with his hand on the hand of one disciple who was going through a series of inner temptations at the time. Master took his hand away, saying, "Hot." That's all he said. He could feel the heat of that disciple's body, caused by the friction built up by this conflict within him.

You'll sometimes feel a cool breeze flowing from saints, actually coming out of their bodies. I remember sitting next to Daya Mata at a banquet one time, and I could feel this cool breeze coming out of her body. It was very soothing and pleasant. These are all different manifestations—the burning skin and so on—of this inner conflict.

"O Krishna, I don't want victory. I don't want a kingdom just for myself. What would I want with all these royal pleasures? What use would all these things be to me? If I were to kill my own people, what a sin!"

"How terrible to kill these qualities in me!" The ego may go to ridiculous extremes in its rationalizations. I'm reminded of that song from "Oklahoma," "I'm Just a Girl Who Can't Say No." She sings, "Whatcha gonna do when a fella acts flirty, starts to talk purtty, whatcha gonna do—spit in his eye?" As if that were the only alternative! (laughter) That's an example of the sort of thing the ego will come up with, the absurd reasons it invents for not doing what it knows it ought to do. Arjuna is saying, "I can't imagine any good that would come from the sin of killing these friends of mine." You think of giving up a desire, and then respond with, "Oh, no, what a terrible thing to do! I'd be sacrificing part of my own consciousness. I'd be half dead!" What's that other song, from "Porgy and Bess"—about Methuselah who lived 900 years, "But there's no use in living when no gal will give in." So what good is 900 years, is the idea.

The thought here is, what's the point of living if I can't have fun, too? And, well, this is the battle that happens for all devotees. They reach that middle point and they say "Oh, no, not that, anything else. Ask me to give up ice cream—I don't like ice cream." (laughter) And Arjuna says, "... and those for whose sake we covet the throne and luxuries." He's describing heavenly joy and saying, "But egotistically to want divine joy, egotistically to want love and so on, just for me when I've got these other things to take care of? Why, that's wrong, wrong!" (laughter)

And so Arjuna sits there, and he gets very discouraged and says, "O Krishna, I don't want to kill them. Even if they kill me, I will be noble, I won't kill. Even for the sovereignty of the three worlds, how then for sovereignty on this earth? Krishna, what joy can we derive through slaying the sons of Dhritarashtra? Sin only will come to us if we kill these desperadoes. Therefore, Krishna, it does not behoove us to kill our own relations. How shall we be happy if we kill our own? If we can't be loyal to our own, how can we be loyal to anybody else?"

So, with all sorts of rationalizations, the struggle goes on. It may be one kind of rationalization or it may be another, but you listen to people talking as long as I have and you begin to hear quite a few different reasons for doing the wrong things. They all sound very good and self-righteous, but as Master said once, "People are so skillful in their ignorance." They have so many good reasons for doing what they shouldn't do.

"And so, although these people with minds blinded by greed do not perceive the evil of destroying one's own race, and the sin occurring from enmity towards sin, why shouldn't we, O Krishna, who see clearly the sin involved in the destruction of one's family, think of turning away from this crime?"

He goes on like this. Finally, at the end of Chapter One, he says: "Arjuna, with his mind agitated by grief on the battlefield, having spoken thus, and having laid down his bow..."—given up meditating, in other words—"...and arrows..."—arrows means the energy that you shoot upwards; giving up the arrows means you just can't send that energy up any more, you just sort of let it sag for awhile, "...and then sank into the hinder part of his chariot..."—sat back. What's the hinder part? Well, it's obvious, isn't it? (laughter) You sink back into the lower centers. "Oh, it's too much trouble." You go back into the worldly consciousness—outward consciousness, in other words.

And so, Chapter Two begins, and Arjuna says, "No, I just won't fight." Then Krishna says to him, "But Arjuna, how has this infatuation overtaken you at this odd hour?" This is really something to remember, it's an important point. I experienced it, maybe you've all had the chance to experience it, too; but if you haven't yet, you will. You get a certain degree of calmness, and that's when the struggles get harder. First of all there's that thought, "I feel calm; I feel so good, nothing could take me away." That's when it suddenly happens.

Anandamayee Ma, a great Indian saint about whom Paramhansa Yogananda wrote a chapter in his *Autobiography*, puts it this way. You go out with a raft and try to get into the ocean of Spirit. You come to one point in the beach and you get into the water, and then the waves beat you back. And so you say, "Okay, that's not the right place to go in." And then you go down the beach a bit, and you make another effort, and again the waves beat you back; and this happens again and again, and finally you find a place where the water no longer beats you back, and you just get taken by the water out to sea.

So in the beginning it's a matter of constant struggle, until, as Master put it, "efforts end in ease." After a while it becomes natural, there's no struggle involved. But in the beginning—and the beginning can last incarnations, my dears; it doesn't have to but it can...Don't think, "Oh, he's been meditating fifty years and he hasn't got God yet." He may not get God for several times fifty years. What does it matter how long it takes, as long as there's only that to be found? Somebody said to me last night, "Oh, what long discipline is involved!" Well, life itself is long, so why not live in the right way? As Master put it, we have to live anyway, so why not live in such a way as to find joy?

But the truth is that you *can* get out in this lifetime if you work at it—especially, Master said, with the practice of Kriya Yoga, which gets that energy flowing right where the battlefield is, in the spine. When you can bring that energy there strongly, it dissolves all those things and then you become free. You can get out in this lifetime, though it isn't easy. It takes a long time, usually; but you've already come a long way just to be here. A long way. You wouldn't be wanting these truths if you hadn't been practicing these things before. So take courage from that, and say, "Maybe this is the life when I can really kick the bucket and get out."

Krishna is saying to Arjuna, "this odd hour"—the meaning here being that you are sitting in absolute peace and calmness, and that's when you should soar; and right then is when all those reminders come—"Ooooooh, that city was pretty nice!" and so on. I've seen also that when people come to Ananda, often the newcomers will be thinking a lot about what they've come from; but then they get out of that thought, and they get immersed in what they're doing in a positive way. The same thing happens here in meditation.

"It is shunned by noble souls. Neither will it bring you heaven, nor fame, nor anything that you may want. You won't find what you're looking for if you talk in this way. This is false reasoning. Don't yield to unmanliness, it becomes you ill. Shake off this paltry faint-heartedness. Arise, O Scorcher of Enemies!" He's trying to encourage him. Arjuna says, "How, Krishna, shall I fight Bhishma and Drona with arrows? They are both objects of reverence. O Destroyer of Foes, it is better to live on alms in this world without slaying anybody, because even after killing them we shall enjoy only blood-stained pleasures in the form of wealth and sense enjoyments. We don't know which is preferable for us, to fight or not to fight. Nor do we know whether we shall win, or whether they shall conquer us. The sons of Dhritarashtra, by killing whom we do not even wish to live, are arrayed against us, that, my very being tainted by the vice of faint-heartedness, and my mind puzzled with regard to duty, I'm asking you, tell me that which is decidedly good. I am Your disciple, pray, instruct me, who have sought refuge in You. So even on obtaining undisputed sovereignty, and an affluent kingdom on this earth and lordship over the gods, I do not see any means which can drive away the grief which is drying up my senses." Sanjaya said, "O King, having thus spoken to Sri Krishna, Arjuna again said to him, 'I will not fight,' and became silent. Then, O Dhritarashtra, Sri Krishna as if smiling addressed the following words..."

Now, that smile: Here's what happens. That faintheartedness comes along many times on the path, but when you've struggled long enough, finally you reach the point where God comes sweetly and takes you away. There's a story in the life of St. Teresa of Avila, who after many, many tests and many temptations, saw this young man who wanted to win her to himself; and so was friendly toward him, until suddenly she saw Christ right by the man's side. She could see him; the man couldn't; and she became so completely fixed on Christ's image that she couldn't even speak to this man any more. The man tried to get her to speak, and finally just got discouraged and left. But Master said that when you've advanced a certain distance on the path, God will protect you; God will manifest Himself openly and take you out. In this case, St. Teresa had gone though so many tests that she had proved her love, really, and so God came and took that test away from her.

Remember that He is on your side, and He will protect you. "Sri Krishna, as if smiling..."—to see the smile of God, to see the smile of that inner light is something that comes to the devotee when he's already reached a certain level of advancement; he's no beginner by any means, at this point. And then he sees that God smilingly says, "Now come along." He begins to bless him and change everything for him. At first it seems as if we're alone, but then suddenly we find that He is there, and He is helping us. At first it seems that He's very silent and not taking part in the battle, but then He steps in and says, "Look, I am with you." As Jesus puts it, "I am with you always."

"Arjuna, you grieve over those who should not be grieved for, and yet you speak like the learned." You see, you're just playing with words, but what you're saying is wrong. Now this is true on different levels, and I'll talk about it more in a few minutes. "Wise men do not sorrow over the dead or the living. In fact, there was never a time when I was not, nor you, or these kings were not. Nor is it a fact that hereafter we shall all cease to be. Just as boyhood, youth, and old age are attributed to the soul through this body, even so it attains another body. The wise man does not get deluded about all this." In other words, you take off the body the way you take off an overcoat, the *Gita* says.

There's a story that somebody reminded me of just a few minutes ago, that I've also enjoyed in the past. A wealthy man went to a psychic to find out who he would be in his next incarnation, so that he could will all his money to that person. (laughter) The wish to take it with you is, of course, strong, but it is not possible. We take off this garment and everything belonging to it, but *we* don't die. *We* continue to live.

Murder is wrong basically for this spiritual reason, that it means a wrong mental affirmation on your part. Remember that you are really dealing with your own self; outward sin is bad primarily for what it does to you. If it's that person's *karma* to be murdered or killed, he'll be killed in some way. It's wrong for *you* to do it. As

Jesus said, "It must needs be that evils come, but woe unto them through whom they come." So the thing that's wrong about murder has less to do with what it does to the other person—his *karma* is acting, and will act in any case—but it's more a matter of what it's doing to you. It's an affirmation in your own mind of the destruction of life; it's a rejection of life, or an effort to destroy some aspect of it—in the last analysis, some aspect of *your own* life, because whatever you don't like in others is always a reflection of something that you don't in yourself.

This is axiomatic: Any fault that people judge or condemn in others is a fault in their own nature as well. If it weren't in themselves, they wouldn't be intolerant of it. They would see it, but it wouldn't upset them. Always, therefore, if you find yourself feeling intolerant of someone, use that intolerance as a guide to what you need to overcome in yourself. It doesn't mean that if you're pure and perfect, you become blind to the darkness in others. You can see it much more clearly; but you don't condemn it; you are people's friend; you want to help them to get out of darkness. So, this objectification that makes you want to destroy someone is really making you want to destroy something in yourself. It's an aspect of suicide; you're trying to kill some part of yourself. That's why an even greater sin than murder is to kill yourself. The greatest sin, in fact, is suicide, because it means the denial of life itself. If we want to grow spiritually, we must understand that, in objective reality, life and death are all the same thing.

Master one time talked to me about how God "eats people"; meaning, God doesn't really care whether we live or die, physically, because He sees that you can't die anyway. Whether you're in this body or out of it, you're still that same spark of His consciousness. Out of compassion, if you pray to Him, He may help you to live longer here on earth, but He sees in Himself that there is no death.

So when a soldier kills on the battlefield, what makes it right depends upon his consciousness. What I'm saying, essentially, is that there is a justification sometimes for killing in righteous war, or killing for a righteous cause, if you're doing it as an affirmation of life, not of death.

Good and evil are always at war. You know, we talk about Christ and his forgiveness on the cross and how nonviolent he was and so on; but remember how he took a whip to those money changers in the temple? He used the appropriate method to enable goodness to win out over evil. There is always going to be a war between the two, and what makes a violent conflict wrong is when the motives are wrong, when there's hatred.

Obviously, in a war if you can win with love, all the better, but there are times—for example, when there is one person who is destroying many people—where it may be necessary to punish him, to put him in prison, even to kill him in a fight rather than allow hundreds of people to be killed. In this case it's not an affirmation of his death; if you do it with the right consciousness, you're doing it with compassion for him, but with a greater compassion, a greater awareness of the need of these people to survive, the many innocent women and children, rather than this one vicious criminal.

So sometimes we have a choice, because always in this

world we are faced with relativity. Sometimes it's a choice between the lesser of two evils, and we haven't a choice of an absolute good. If we can win him with love, if we have that kind of power, fine; but there's no point in trying to exercise a kind of power that you don't have. In that case you must recognize that there is a battle between good and evil. As Master put it, if a bandit comes to your home and threatens your family, and you, while running out the back door, say, "I forgive you for anything that you may do to my dear ones," you're being a coward. That's not non-violence.

There is always the need to do battle with evil, but in a good way, the best way that you can come up with; and always, the motive should be right. So you see, what Krishna says is true even on a physical level. Not, of course, that every war is righteous, just because you're fighting it. But there *are* times, clearly, when truth demands some kind of outward, physical manifestation.

Yet at the same time, what Krishna is really talking about here is the struggle between our own higher and lower qualities. What he's saying is that our lower qualities can't be destroyed. Let's take, for instance, a desire for ice cream. It's not a bad desire; I'm just offering it as an example of a physical desire. If you end up not wanting that ice cream, it doesn't mean you've killed a part of your own self. All it means is that you've taken the energy that you would have directed toward that, and redirected it to something else.

The same amount of energy is committed to myriads of things, desires for things, people, places, and so on. Each one of these is not yourself, it's merely a commitment of your energy; and when you can release this energy, then you find that you have *more* energy, not less—more energy to do the things that will really give you happiness.

If you give up the desire for greed or hatred, it doesn't mean that you become half a man. The proof of what I'm saying is that those who have transmuted their desires are *more* human; they are more alive. That same energy that went toward greed has become redirected toward nonattachment and joy, toward an affirmation of completeness in the Self, toward the practice of contentment, and so on. So Krishna, in saying that there is no death, that a person who dies in this form merely gets born into a new form, means that the energy that you commit into one particular mental trait becomes "born again" in a new mental trait. You won't kill anything in yourself by getting rid of your bad qualities.

Now, this is what you need to tell yourself when you are doing inner battle, when you are on the battlefield of inner conflict between your worldly desires and your spiritual aspirations. The mind says, "Oh, I can't possibly give *that* up!" But remember, you're not really giving anything up. You're merely putting your energy into something that will give you joy, instead of misery.

This is the key to the *Bhagavad Gita*. I could go on all day and all night on the subject; but here at least is the key; it gives you the right approach. From here on, as you read the *Bhagavad Gita*, you will see that everything that Krishna says refers primarily to the *inner* divine search. Approaching the *Gita* in this way, you'll find wonderful teachings.

For example, there is a lovely passage that Paramhansa Yogananda talks about briefly. Krishna says,

"If you give up your battle, Arjuna, then all those people who have looked up to you will hold you in contempt." It's psychological fact, isn't it? that when you lose a psychological battle, your mind sits back and scorns you— "Oh, look at you! You've done it again!" Isn't it so? A part of your mind looks at you with contempt; it's a psychological fact of human nature. All these things that he's talking about deal with our own psychology. Read the *Bhagavad Gita* in this light, and it will give you tremendous fruit for meditation and spiritual growth.

When Master's book comes out, I think we will begin to see what he meant when he said, "Millions will find God through this book." He didn't mean that they'd go into *samadhi* after reading the book, but that it would give them the understanding that would help them to follow the true path.

I have read or glanced at so much garbage in modern literature, even by some of the teachers from India, where they will say things that have nothing to do with these truths. You read those things and you just get confused. This book of Master's will give you the truth. I'm not being sectarian. The fact of it is that nobody can come up with a *new* truth. When some people say things that are totally at variance with truth as it has been taught since the most ancient of days, you'll see that it is not true. Everything one teaches, even though it is put in new ways, has to be in keeping with that ancient tradition.

Something I honor in Master is that he always referred back whatever he taught to the ancient teachings. For truth never changes: It is ever new. I asked him once if he had brought a new religion. "It is a new *expression* of religion," he replied—a new expression, in other words, of *Sanatan Dharma*, of that eternal religion. There can't be a wholly new religion, a wholly new teaching. Until people understand this basic fact, what they teach will be outward.

I've been amazed at the things that people have written, even great scholars, on the *Bhagavad Gita*—describing it in terms that don't relate to our inner life, to our relationship with God, and making it sound as if it were only about outward rites and practices. No, *this* is the reality of the *Gita*: It is the story of your own inner self, of your own aspiration toward the Divine, and how to win the battle with your lower nature.

The message of the *Gita* is to bring you into an understanding of life as a constant battle, until the war is won for the forces of eternal bliss.

ABOUT THE AUTHOR

J. Donald Walters (who later received the monastic name Kriyananda) was born in 1926 in Rumania, to American parents. He was educated in Rumania, Switzerland, England, and the United States, viewing Western civilization from both sides of the ocean.

At an early age he decided to become an author and playwright, but later abandoned the ambition, not because he lacked ability, but because he felt unable to say anything truly *meaningful*.

In *The Path: A Spiritual Autobiography*, Kriyananda describes his intense and moving search for meaning. This search culminated in 1948 when he met and became a direct disciple of Paramhansa Yogananda, the famous master of yoga. For fourteen years he served his master's organization, Self-Realization Fellowship, as director of SRF centers around the world, principal teacher and lecturer, member of the Board of Directors, and first vice-president.

Having been instructed by Yogananda to serve others specifically through writing and teaching, Kriyananda returned to his literary endeavors. Since 1962 he has written many books, short stories, plays, and poems. Each of these approaches the question of life's deeper meaning from a different perspective: philosophy (*Crises in Modern Thought*); sociology (*Intentional Communities*); psychology and astrology (*Your Sun Sign as a Spiritual Guide*); art (*The Artist as a Channel*); drama and humor (*The Jewel in the Lotus*); and the classic science of yoga (*Yoga Postures for Higher Awareness* and *14 Steps to*

Higher Awareness).

In addition to his writing, Kriyananda is also well known for the power and quality of his voice, both as a speaker and a singer. A prolific composer, he has written original spiritual music for voice, piano, and chorus. One of his current directions is "spiritualizing the arts."

In 1968, Kriyananda founded Ananda World Brotherhood Village, one of the first and most successful new spiritual communities in the world. At present, Kriyananda lives at Ananda, where he continues his work of writing and teaching. He also spends increasingly more time lecturing throughout North America and abroad.

A Selection of Other Books by Kriyananda (J. Donald Walters)

"Secrets" series — daily thoughts for the month ($4.95 each):

Secrets of Happiness
Secrets of Success
Secrets of Attracting and Keeping Friends
Secrets of Persuasion
Secrets of Meditation
Secrets of Inner Peace
Secrets of Overcoming Harmful Emotions

Affirmations and Prayers — a collection of 52 spiritual qualities and a discussion of each, with an affirmation and prayer for its realization. $7.95

Yoga Postures for Higher Awareness — This unique book teaches hatha yoga as it was originally intended: as a way to uplift your consciousness and aid your spiritual development. $9.95

Rays of the Same Light — Parallel Passages, with Commentary, from the Bible and the Bhagavad Gita. (3 vols., $9.95 each)

Your Sun Sign as a Spiritual Guide. $7.95

The Essence of Self-Realization: The Wisdom of Paramhansa Yogananda. Meet one of this century's greatest spiritual teachers through his spoken words. $9.95

Cities of Light — What communities can accomplish, and the need for them in our times. $7.95

Crises in Modern Thought — Solutions to the Problem of Meaninglessness. This book probes the discoveries of modern science for their pertinence to lasting human values. $11.95

The Path: A Spiritual Autobiography. Kriyananda recounts those events in his life which lead up to and include his years of training under the great master Paramhansa Yogananda. $6.95

ORDER FORM

CRYSTAL CLARITY, PUBLISHERS specializes in self–help and psychology books. For a complete listing of our products, send for a Crystal Clarity catalogue.

Quantity	Item	Price
_____	_____	_____
_____	_____	_____
_____	_____	_____
_____	_____	_____
_____	_____	_____

6% tax in California _____

Shipping: $2.00 for 1 or 2 items; $3 for more _____

TOTAL _____

Please send payment and order to Crystal Clarity, 14618 Tyler Foote Road, Nevada City, CA 95959. Call toll free (800) 424-1055.

Name _____

Address _____

City _____ State ___ Zip _____

Phone _____

Please charge to my credit card# _____

☐ VISA ☐ MasterCard Exp. Date _____